THE
TOTALLY
SHRIMP
COOKBOOK

THE TOTALLY SHRIMP COOKBOOK

By Helene Siegel

Illustrated by Carolyn Vibbert

CELESTIAL ARTS
BERKELEY, CALIFORNIA

The Totally Shrimp Cookbook is produced by becker&mayer!, Ltd.

Printed in Singapore.

Cover design and illustration: Dick Witt
Interior design and typesetting: Susan Hernday
Interior illustrations: Carolyn Vibbert

Library of Congress Cataloging-in-Publication Data
Siegel, Helene.
The Totally Shrimp Cookbook / by Helene Siegel.
    p.   cm.
ISBN 0-89087-823-4
1. Cookery (Shrimp)   I. Title.
TX754.S58S54   1997
641.6'95—dc21   96-45672
                                                   CIP

Celestial Arts Publishing
P.O. Box 7123
Berkeley, CA 94707

Other cookbooks in this series:
The Totally Crab Cookbook
The Totally Lobster Cookbook
The Totally Salmon Cookbook

TO SEAFOOD LOVERS EVERYWHERE

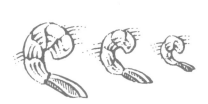

CONTENTS

INTRODUCTION

Shrimp are as sweet and innocent as their name would suggest. And as easy as anything to cook.

They are always available at the supermarket, where quality and price are fairly consistent. Shrimp are easy to peel, quick to cook, low in fat with a good dose of protein, and they turn a lovely pink color when done.

Add to these the facts that they taste wonderful either hot or cold, and combine well with fiery flavors from the Far East, Louisiana, and Mexico; salty flavors from Japan and China; sweet fruits, coconut, and barbecue of the Caribbean; garlic and pasta from Italy; or just plain butter from France; and you realize that shrimp are an extraordinary gift from the sea. We Americans were exercising extreme good taste and pure logic when we made shrimp the most popular seafood in our country.

In return, this simple crustacean doesn't ask for much. All it wants is to be eaten while still fresh, cooked briefly, and shared with an appreciative audience. Here then are some recipes to get the good times rolling.

And remember, though shrimp are the cocktail food par excellence, everybody deserves an occasional weeknight shrimp dinner at home—for the pure pleasure of it.

TANTALIZING
APPETIZERS

BACON SHRIMP BITES

Here is divine finger food for the hopelessly hedonistic: one perfect, plump shrimp wrapped up in succulent bacon.

1 pound large shrimp, shelled and
   deveined
¾ pound sliced bacon, slices halved
honey mustard for dipping

Preheat oven to 400 degrees F.

Wrap a half bacon slice around each shrimp in a spiral to enclose. Pierce with a toothpick to hold. Arrange on a baking sheet and bake 10 to 12 minutes, until bacon is done. Drain on paper towels and serve, hot or room temperature, with honey mustard for dipping.

MAKES ABOUT 24 PIECES

HOT PAPRIKA SHRIMP

Paprika, the ground spice from dried red pepper pods, shares a special affinity with sweet shrimp. Serving the shrimp in the shell adds a bit of crunch to this simple, elegant dish.

½ pound large shrimp, in the shell
salt, freshly ground pepper, and paprika
3 tablespoons butter
2 teaspoons cognac or brandy
1 bunch watercress, stems trimmed
lemon juice for sprinkling

Pat the shrimp dry and spread on a large sheet of waxed paper or a towel. Sprinkle generously with salt, pepper, and paprika. Gather up the paper and shake the shrimp to coat evenly.

Melt the butter in a large skillet over medium-high heat. When nearly brown, add the shrimp. Cook, shaking the pan frequently, until shrimp are evenly pink and curled, about 2 minutes. Add the cognac and remove from heat.

Arrange the watercress on 4 serving plates. Sprinkle with lemon juice, salt, and pepper. Top each with shrimp in the shell.

SERVES 4

How to Prepare Shrimp

Shrimp are the easiest shellfish for the cook to handle. To peel, simply remove the shells with your fingertips. The shells are about the thickness of cellophane and grow in segments. Leave the last segment on, along with the tail, for recipes specifying tail on. Then rinse with cold water and refrigerate. Save peeled shells in zipper-lock bags in the freezer for making shrimp stock (see page 46) or enriching other stocks and soups. Shrimp shells are entirely edible—a chef I know considers them an excellent source of calcium—and they add an element of crunch, not to mention fiber, to the diet.

GAZPACHO SHRIMP COCKTAIL

This marriage of two summertime favorites—gazpacho and shrimp cocktail—is a sure winner for hot-weather dinner parties. Double or triple the recipe for buffets.

1 small tomato, seeded and diced
1 small cucumber, peeled, seeded, and diced
½ green bell pepper, cored, seeded, and diced
¼ cup diced red onion
¼ cup chopped fresh cilantro
1½ cups tomato juice
¼ cup red wine vinegar
juice of 2 limes
1 teaspoon sugar
2 dashes Worcestershire sauce
4 dashes Tabasco sauce
salt and freshly ground pepper
½ pound cooked, peeled medium shrimp

In a large bowl, combine tomato, cucumber, green pepper, onion, and cilantro.

In another bowl, whisk together tomato juice, vinegar, lime juice, sugar, Worcestershire, and Tabasco. Season with salt and pepper to taste. Pour over the chopped vegetables. Cut the shrimp into large chunks. Add to the vegetable mixture and mix well. Cover with plastic wrap and chill 2 hours. Serve cold with tortilla chips.

SERVES 4

The big fish eat the little ones, the little ones eat the shrimp, and the shrimp are forced to eat mud.
            —*Chinese proverb*

WONTON SHRIMP

In these minimal wontons, a single shrimp is wrapped and then fried. Very easy for holding in one hand while balancing a cold cocktail in the other.

1 pound medium shrimp, shelled
    and deveined
salt and freshly ground pepper
36 wonton wrappers
½ cup fresh cilantro leaves
peanut oil for frying
assorted mustards, spicy cocktail sauce,
    or soy sauce for dipping

Pat the shrimp dry, and season all over with salt and pepper.

Place a wonton wrapper on the counter and place a cilantro leaf in the center. Top with a shrimp and another leaf. Moisten two adjoining edges of wrapper with a finger dipped in cold water. Fold over the dry edges to form a triangle and press to seal. Then moisten the triangle's tip with water, fold over, and press to form a crescent. Set aside. Repeat with the rest of the shrimp.

Bring about 3 cups of oil to deep-fry temperature in a fryer or deep pot. Test oil by dropping in a strip of wonton skin. If it immediately bubbles to the surface, the oil is ready. Fry, a handful at a time, until golden brown, about 2 minutes total. Remove with slotted spoon and drain on paper towels. Serve hot with dipping sauces.

MAKES ABOUT 30 PIECES

CAJUN POPCORN

With a salute to Paul Prudhomme, the Cajun master, here is a variation on his famous Louisiana cocktail food.

1 egg
½ cup plus 2 tablespoons milk
¾ cup flour
½ teaspoon sugar
½ teaspoon salt
¼ teaspoon garlic powder
¼ teaspoon cayenne
¼ teaspoon black pepper
¼ teaspoon dried thyme
vegetable oil for frying
1 pound rock shrimp, peeled and thawed

Whisk together the egg and milk in a small bowl.

In a large bowl, combine the flour with sugar and spices. Add the milk mixture and whisk until thoroughly blended. Let sit at room temperature 1 hour.

Pour oil to a depth of 1 inch in a large skillet and heat to 350 degrees F. Add the shrimp, a small handful at a time, to the batter and toss to coat evenly. Fry in batches until golden brown all over, 1 to 3 minutes total. Remove with slotted spoon and drain on paper towels. Serve hot with any of the cold dipping sauces.

SERVES 6

HOT SHRIMP WITH
SOY SCALLION DIP

Sometimes a messy dish like this is all a party really needs to get off on the right casual note.

1 pound large or medium shrimp,
   in the shell
3 tablespoons soy sauce
1 teaspoon rice wine vinegar
3 scallions, white and green, thinly sliced
1 tablespoon peanut oil
¼ teaspoon chile oil
1 teaspoon salt

Bring a large pot of water to a boil. Rinse the shrimp in cold water.

Meanwhile, in a small serving bowl, combine the soy sauce, vinegar, and scallions. Combine the peanut and chile oil in a small pan and heat over medium heat about 3 minutes. Pour into the scallion mixture.

Add the salt and shrimp to the boiling water and cook, uncovered, 3 minutes. Drain and transfer hot shrimp to serving bowl. Bring to the table with dip and a bowl for the shells.

SERVES 6

How to Prepare Shrimp

To devein shrimp—that is, remove the black intestinal vein that runs along the back—you must first peel them. Then, holding the shrimp in one hand, run a sharp paring knife along the outside curve and slice about 1/4-inch down. Remove the vein under cold, running water. The main reason for deveining shrimp is aesthetic, since the vein is not harmful to eat. In some regions of the country, it is ordinarily left in. I became a vein-eating convert (to no ill effect) while testing the recipes for this book. Peeling is always optional.

Butterflying shrimp means splitting them lengthwise and pressing them open to lie flat. It can be done with or without removing shells.

ROCK SHRIMP SEVICHE

This elegant Mexican marinated fish dish is adapted from a recipe in Mesa Mexicana *by chefs Mary Sue Milliken and Susan Feniger.*

1 pound rock or small shrimp, briefly
    boiled and peeled
1 small red onion, diced
1 serrano chile, seeded and finely diced
1 bunch cilantro, chopped
½ cup fish stock
¼ cup lime juice
1 teaspoon salt
tortilla chips for serving

Combine all of the ingredients in a glass or ceramic bowl, and mix well. Cover and chill thoroughly. Serve with tortilla chips.

SERVES 6

COLD MARINATED GREEK SHRIMP

1 pound large shrimp, in the shell
6 garlic cloves, minced
1/3 cup lemon juice
1/3 cup olive oil
2 tablespoons chopped fresh oregano or parsley
1 teaspoon grated lemon zest
salt and freshly ground pepper

Bring a large pot of water to a boil. Add pinch of salt and the shrimp, and cook about 2 minutes, until orange-pink. Drain and set aside to cool. When cool enough to handle, remove shells and cut shrimp in half lengthwise, removing vein.

Whisk together garlic, lemon juice, olive oil, oregano, and lemon zest in a large bowl. Add shrimp, salt, and pepper, and toss to combine. Chill and serve.

SERVES 6

SHRIMP IN LETTUCE CUPS

Stir-fried bits of shrimp and vegetables served in crisp lettuce leaves.

1 head iceberg lettuce
½ pound large shrimp, peeled and cut
    into 5 slices
2½ tablespoons soy sauce
2 tablespoons dry sherry
salt and freshly ground pepper
1 tablespoon oyster sauce
1 teaspoon mirin (sweet rice wine)
¼ teaspoon sesame oil
2 tablespoons vegetable oil
2 teaspoons minced garlic
6 small dried shiitake mushroom caps,
    reconstituted and chopped
1 carrot, peeled and diced
¼ cup bean sprouts
2 scallions, white and green, thinly sliced

Cut lettuce in half close to the core.

Carefully peel outer leaves so 8 pieces can be used as serving cups. Reserve.

Combine shrimp, 2 tablespoons of the soy sauce, 1 tablespoon of the sherry, salt, and pepper in a small bowl. Marinate 15 minutes. Meanwhile, in another small bowl, mix together the remaining soy sauce and sherry with oyster sauce, mirin, and sesame oil.

Heat a medium skillet at high setting. Add 1 tablespoon of the vegetable oil, and whirl to coat the pan. Lift shrimp from marinade, shaking off excess, and add to hot pan with garlic. Stir-fry just until pink. Transfer to platter.

Add remaining tablespoon of oil to pan. Add mushrooms, carrot, bean sprouts, and scallions, and stir-fry less than 1 minute. Pour in reserved sauce mixture and shrimp. Stir-fry about 1 minute and remove. Spoon into lettuce cups and serve.

SERVES 4

SHRIMP AND VEGETABLE SPRING ROLLS

It is worth a trip to a specialty Asian market for paper-thin spring roll wrappers. Unlike wontons, they do not need any cooking, and they can be used to wrap a myriad of salad ingredients into instant hot-weather hors d'oeuvres.

1 (2-ounce) bunch dried bean threads
about 10 Vietnamese spring roll wrappers, thawed and kept moist
½ pound medium shrimp, cooked and peeled
½ cup julienned carrots
2 cups bean sprouts
14 basil or mint leaves, cut in half if large

HONEY LIME DIP
½ cup lime juice
2 tablespoons honey
1 tablespoon Thai fish sauce
¼ teaspoon Chinese hot chile oil

Place the bean threads in a bowl with enough boiling water to cover. Let sit 15 minutes to soften. Drain and cut into 2-inch lengths.

One at a time, place a wrapper on a counter in a diamond shape. Have ready a bowl of cold water for dipping and wrappers tucked under a moistened kitchen towel. Place 5 or 6 shrimp in a horizontal line in the center of the wrapper, leaving 1½ inches bare at the corners. Top the shrimp with a thin layer of carrots and then bean sprouts. Cover with a generous portion of bean threads. Top with a layer of basil.

To fold, moisten all the outside edges with water. Lift the bottom point, and tuck it up and over to tightly enclose the filling. Fold one side over, moistening if dry, and tightly roll to seal, leaving one edge open. Stir together Honey Lime Dip ingredients in a serving bowl. Serve.

MAKES 8 TO 10 ROLLS

SHRIMP SKEWERS
WITH BURNT ORANGE

*If using wood, presoak skewers in cold water
and place in the freezer for a few hours before
grilling, to minimize charring.*

1 cup olive oil
grated zest of 1 orange
grated zest of 2 lemons
1 teaspoon red pepper flakes
2 teaspoons minced garlic
½ pound large shrimp, peeled
2 small oranges, halved and
   cut in 8 small wedges
½ red bell pepper, cored, seeded,
   and cut in 1-inch chunks
½ small red onion, cut in 1-inch chunks
   and rings separated
salt

Whisk together the olive oil, orange and lemon zest, red pepper flakes, and garlic in a shallow plastic container.

Thread the skewers with shrimp, orange wedges, and chunks of pepper and onion, beginning and ending with an orange. Place in container with marinade and chill 1 to 4 hours, spooning occasionally with marinade.

To cook, preheat broiler or grill. Cook, turning frequently and brushing with marinade, until shrimp are pink all over, about 5 minutes. Season with salt and serve.

SERVES 3

PICKLED SHRIMP

This adaptation of traditional Southern-style spiced, pickled shrimp is delicious served with small triangles of good buttered bread—preferably rye or pumpernickel.

water
3 teaspoons salt
2 tablespoons Old Bay seasoning
1 pound medium shrimp, peeled with
    tails on
1/2 cup red wine vinegar
1/2 cup olive oil
1/2 teaspoon freshly ground black pepper
1/2 teaspoon sugar
1/4 teaspoon red chile flakes
1 teaspoon fennel seeds
2 bay leaves
1 lemon, thinly sliced
6 scallions, white part, thinly sliced

Bring a large pot of water to a boil.
Add 2 teaspoons salt, Old Bay, and shrimp.
Cook 2 minutes (do not return to a boil).
Drain and transfer to a bowl.

Whisk together red wine vinegar, olive
oil, remaining teaspoon salt, black pepper,
sugar, red chile flakes, and fennel seeds.
Pour over the shrimp. Add the remaining
ingredients, toss well, cover, and refrigerate.
Serve cold.

SERVES 4

STEAMED SHRIMP DUMPLINGS

This is the classic pork and shrimp combination served in Cantonese restaurants.

½ pound medium shrimp, shelled
   and roughly chopped
1 egg white
4 dried shiitakes, soaked in hot water
   15 minutes, stemmed and minced
¼ cup finely chopped jicama
1 teaspoon minced fresh ginger
4 scallions, white and green, finely
   chopped
1 tablespoon dry sherry
2 teaspoons soy sauce
¼ teaspoon sugar
½ teaspoon Chinese hot chile oil
about 24 round wonton wrappers
peanut oil for coating

Combine the shrimp, egg white, shiitakes, jicama, ginger, scallions, dry sherry, soy sauce, sugar, and hot chile oil in a bowl. Mix well.

On a counter, with a bowl of cold water nearby, arrange the wonton wrappers. Place about 1 tablespoon of filling in the center of each and moisten the edges with cold water. To seal, gather the tops in one hand and lift, squeezing the top in the curve between thumb and index finger, forming pleats. With the other hand, tamp down filling at top and flatten bottom. Lightly coat with oil and place on steamer basket or plate on rack.

Place in steamer with 1 inch water. Bring to a boil, cover, and reduce heat to medium. Cook about 10 minutes, until pork is no longer pink. Serve hot with dips.

MAKES 24

SHRIMP COCKTAIL
WITH TWO DIPS

Who can resist shrimp cocktail? I, personally, have never tried. The key to getting this simple dish just right is taking care not to overcook the shrimp, serving it chilled but not for too long—the shrimp must be fresh—and having a few enticing dips to choose from. Just make sure to prepare more than enough, since ice-cold shrimp on a buffet has a tendency to disappear quickly.

To boil shrimp for cocktail, use extra-large or jumbo shrimp in the shell. Bring a large pot of salted water to a boil. Add the shrimp and start timing—2 to 3 minutes, until the shells are pink—and drain. Quickly spread on towels in a single layer to drain and cool. Peel when cool enough to handle, leaving tails on. Cover and chill until serving time. Serve with dipping sauces.

SPICY COCKTAIL SAUCE

½ cup ketchup
½ jalapeño chile, seeded and diced
2 tablespoons chopped fresh cilantro
3 tablespoons finely chopped red onion
1 tablespoon lime juice
salt and freshly ground pepper

Mix ingredients together in a bowl and chill.

MAKES ½ CUP

REMOULADE SAUCE

½ cup mayonnaise
2 tablespoons ketchup
1 tablespoon red wine vinegar
2 teaspoons prepared white horseradish
2 tablespoons Dijon mustard
¼ teaspoon paprika
¼ cup minced celery
¼ cup minced red onion
2 tablespoons sweet relish

Combine the ingredients in a small bowl and chill.

MAKES ¾ CUP

SHRIMP SALADS,
SOUPS &
SANDWICHES

TORTILLA SALAD
WITH SPICY SHRIMP

This type of generous main-course salad can be much more delicious at home than at a restaurant, where the shrimp, as a rule, will be smaller and precooked.

1 cup fresh corn kernels, about 1 cob
1 medium head romaine lettuce, washed, dried, and julienned
1 large tomato, cut in small wedges
1 ripe avocado, peeled, pitted, and cut in chunks
½ small red onion, thinly sliced and in rings
¼ cup crumbled feta cheese
vegetable oil for frying
4 corn tortillas, halved and cut into ½-inch strips
1 teaspoon salt
½ teaspoon black pepper

½ teaspoon paprika
¼ teaspoon cayenne
12 ounces large shrimp, in the shell
⅓ cup plus 1 tablespoon lime juice
⅓ cup vegetable oil
salt and freshly ground pepper

Cook the corn in the microwave at full power 1 minute. Combine the lettuce, tomato, avocado, red onion, corn, and feta in a large bowl. Gently toss and chill.

Pour the oil to a depth of about ½ inch in a medium skillet. Heat at medium-high. When hot, add the tortilla strips, a handful at a time. Fry until golden and crisp all over, about 3 minutes. Remove with slotted spoon and drain on paper towels.

Meanwhile, in a small bowl combine the salt, pepper, paprika, and cayenne. Add the shrimp, and toss to coat evenly.

When the tortillas are done, carefully pour out all but about 1 tablespoon of oil from the pan. Return to high heat. Add the shrimp and sauté until orange-pink all over, about 3 minutes. Sprinkle with 1 tablespoon lime juice and remove from heat.

Whisk together the remaining lime juice and vegetable oil. Season to taste with salt and pepper. Pour over the salad and toss well. Transfer to a large serving bowl. Garnish the edges with tortilla strips, spoon the shrimp in the center, and serve.

SERVES 4

CHOPPED SHRIMP SALAD

The classic spread for dainty tea sandwiches or overstuffed kaiser rolls, or for stuffing a ripe avocado or tomato.

¾ pound cooked and peeled bay
   or small shrimp
2 tablespoons mayonnaise
1 tablespoon lemon juice
3 or 4 dashes Tabasco
freshly ground black pepper
1 celery rib, trimmed and diced

Process ½ pound of the shrimp in a food processor until finely chopped. Add mayonnaise, lemon juice, Tabasco, and pepper. Pulse to combine. Transfer to a bowl.

Roughly chop the remaining shrimp and add with celery to mixture. Stir to combine, adjust seasonings, and serve on sandwiches or salads. Store in the refrigerator.

MAKES 1 CUP, ENOUGH FOR 2 LARGE SANDWICHES

MARINATED SHRIMP AND FENNEL SALAD

Here is a refreshing favorite for summer parties.

2 pounds extra-large shrimp in the shell
1 large fennel bulb, trimmed, halved,
   and thinly sliced
1 cup kalamata olives, sliced off pit
½ cup lemon juice
8 garlic cloves, minced
3 tablespoons chopped fresh oregano
   or parsley
½ cup olive oil
salt and freshly ground pepper

Bring a large pot of salted water to a boil.
Cook shrimp until bright orange—about
2 minutes—and drain. Let cool, peel, and
slice in half lengthwise. Combine shrimp in
large bowl with fennel and olives.

In a small bowl, whisk together lemon juice, garlic, oregano, oil, salt, and pepper. Pour over the shrimp mixture, toss well, and adjust with salt and pepper. Chill as long as a day, stirring and tossing occasionally.

SERVES 8 TO 12

Two or Three Things I Know About Shrimp
Always pat shrimp dry and season before frying or sautéing to avoid splatters.

It is always better to err on the side of under-cooking since shrimp are so small. Shrimp start cooking the moment they hit the water or fat. When a recipe gives a time for boiling, start timing imme-diately—do not wait for the water to return to a boil.

Shrimp cooked in the shell retain a bit more flavor and have less chance of overcooking.

WARM SHRIMP SALAD WITH ALMONDS AND ORANGES

An elegant warm salad for formal occasions.

1 medium head butter lettuce, washed
    and torn in bite-size pieces
½ small red onion, thinly sliced
    and separated into rings
½ fennel bulb, thinly sliced crosswise
½ cup roughly chopped roasted almonds
2 tablespoons lemon juice
2 tablespoons olive oil
salt and freshly ground black pepper
1 tablespoon butter
½ pound medium shrimp, peeled
    and deveined
paprika
sections from 2 oranges
3 sprigs thyme, leaves only

Combine the lettuce, red onion, fennel, and almonds in a bowl. Toss and chill.

Whisk together lemon juice, olive oil, salt, and pepper in a small bowl and set aside.

Melt the butter in a medium skillet over medium-high heat. Season the shrimp all over with salt, pepper, and paprika, and add to pan. Sauté until pink all over, about 2 minutes. Add the orange sections, thyme, and reserved lemon dressing. Stir to coat evenly, and cook about 1 minute. Pour over the cold salad, toss, and serve.

SERVES 2 TO 4

SIMPLE SHRIMP STOCK

Store shrimp shells in zipper-lock bags in the freezer for enriching seafood stocks or for making this delicate seafood stock for stews, soups, and sauces.

2 tablespoons butter
2 onions, chopped
shells from 3 pounds shrimp,
    frozen is fine
salt, freshly ground pepper, and paprika
6 cups water

How to Purchase Shrimp

Shrimp are classified according to size and sold by weight. Generally, larger shrimp are more expensive per pound, but the argument could be made that more of their weight is meat rather than shell, thereby evening out the equation. The factor to consider when purchasing shrimp—aside from

Melt the butter in a large, heavy pot over medium heat. Sauté the onions and shrimp shells until pink all over and aromatic, about 10 minutes. Season to taste with salt, pepper, and a pinch of paprika. Pour in the water. Bring to a boil, reduce to a simmer, and cook 45 minutes. Strain through a sieve. Store in a container in the freezer. Keeps for 2 to 3 months.

MAKES 1 QUART

---

apparent freshness—is what size is most appropriate for the dish you plan to cook. Jumbo shrimp with their tails on are great for a luxurious shrimp cocktail or for grilling; medium shrimp out of the shell are preferable for a gumbo to be eaten with spoons.

THAI SOUR SHRIMP SOUP

12 ounces medium shrimp
1 tablespoon vegetable oil
salt
2 serrano chiles, seeded and slivered
2 limes, zest grated, and juiced
2 stalks lemongrass, cut in 2-inch lengths
4 cups chicken stock
2 teaspoons Thai fish sauce or soy sauce
½ bunch chopped cilantro, 3 sliced scallions, 1 red jalapeño chile, seeded and diced as garnish

Peel and devein the shrimp, saving the shells.

Heat the oil in a heavy pot over high heat. Sauté the shells with salt until pink, about 1 minute. Add serranos, lime zest, and lemongrass, and sauté less than 1 minute.

Pour in the chicken stock. Bring to a boil, and simmer 20 minutes. Strain, and pour broth back into pot. Bring to a low boil. Add the shrimp, fish sauce, and lime juice, and cook until shrimp are done, about 2 minutes. Garnish with cilantro, scallions, and jalapeño, and serve hot.

SERVES 4

Shrimp Nutrition

Shrimp, like the other crustaceans, are now thought to be a healthy, high-protein, low-fat food. They are 18 percent protein, 1 percent fat, and 1 percent carbohydrate, with a good dose of B vitamins, phosphorous, iodine, and potassium. They also contain omega-3 fatty fish oils that protect the heart.

CALLALOO WITH SHRIMP

*A true Caribbean callaloo is made from a green
called "dasheen." This one adapts typical island
flavors in a delicate green broth garnished with
sweet shrimp.*

1 quart "Simple Shrimp Stock" (p. 46)
¼ cup long grain rice
1 (10-ounce) package washed spinach
salt, freshly ground pepper,
   and ground nutmeg
1 cup low-fat coconut milk
1 pound medium shrimp, peeled
   and deveined
¼ cup grated, unsweetened coconut as
   garnish (optional)

Combine the shrimp stock and rice in a
soup pot, and bring to a boil. Reduce to a
simmer and cook 15 minutes. Stir in
spinach, turn the heat to high, and cook
about 3 minutes. Season to taste with salt,

pepper, and nutmeg. Transfer to a food processor and purée until smooth. Pour back into the pot.

Add the coconut milk to the broth and bring to a boil. Reduce to a simmer, and stir in shrimp. Cook until shrimp are just done, 3 to 5 minutes. Adjust seasonings. Ladle into bowls, garnish with grated, unsweetened coconut, and serve hot.

SERVES 4

Shrimp Past Their Peak
Shrimp that are starting to spoil have an off smell, with sticky, slimy shells, and possibly black spots on the shell. Once cooked, the meat will be mealy. Be suspicious of shrimp with an ammonia-like odor and yellowing shells. The black spots, called "melanosis," are a sign of aging, and the odor may be sodium bisulfite— a chemical used to retard spoilage.

BARBECUED SHRIMP SANDWICH

Experiment with local brands until you find a favorite barbecue sauce, since regional preferences vary. Then quickly sauté some shrimp, season with sauce, and discover one of life's great pleasures—barbecued shrimp on a bun.

½ pound large shrimp, shelled
   and deveined
salt and freshly ground pepper
1 tablespoon butter
½ cup prepared barbecue sauce,
   preferably sweet
2 kaiser or egg rolls, split and toasted
red onion slices
tomato slices
6 sprigs watercress *or* arugula

Pat shrimp dry, and season all over with salt and pepper. Melt the butter in a small skillet over high heat. Sauté the shrimp until pink all over, about 4 minutes. Add ¼ cup of the barbecue sauce, stir and toss to coat evenly, and remove from heat.

To make sandwiches, coat both sides of toasted roll with barbecue sauce. Divide the shrimp, and layer on sandwich bottoms. Top with onion, tomato slices, and watercress or arugula. Close and cut in half.

MAKES 2

A (Very) Short History of Shrimp

The popularity of shrimp on the American dinner table can be traced directly to the introduction of refrigeration at the turn of the last century. Since they die almost immediately upon exposure to the air and decay quickly afterward, shrimp were once a regional delicacy you had to travel to places like New Orleans to eat. At the same time that refrigeration was being perfected, the American fishing industry began designing nets for harvesting this previously ignored seafood.

In 1902 a Sicilian-American fisherman in Florida, Sollecito Salvador, designed a net that could be pulled by a powerboat. Ten years later commercial fishermen in North Carolina improved upon Salvador's design, but it took another 40 years for deep-sea trawlers to start working the abundant waters off the Atlantic and Gulf coasts.

ROCK TACOS

Rock shrimp, the tiny warm-water shrimp from Florida, are available already peeled, cooked or raw, at specialty markets. They are much tastier than comparable tiny bay shrimp.

½ pound peeled, frozen rock shrimp
4 or 8 corn tortillas
½ cup prepared tomato salsa
1 cup shredded iceberg lettuce
¼ cup diced red onion
1 avocado, in large chunks
freshly ground black pepper
2 limes, cut in wedges

Bring a medium saucepan of salted water to a boil. Add shrimp and cook 3 minutes for frozen or 1 minute for thawed (beginning when shrimp are added). Drain and set aside to cool.

Heat the tortillas, wrapped in foil, in a 350-degree oven 10 minutes.

To make tacos, stack 2 tortillas for each, or if thick, use only one. Spread 2 tablespoons of salsa in the center of each. Top with lettuce, shrimp, onion, and avocado. Season generously with pepper, and serve with lime wedges for seasoning.

MAKES 4

It's a Shrimp's Life
The life cycle of a shrimp is short and sweet.
After the female lays her thousand or so eggs,
they hatch within a day. The microscopic larvae
then drift along on ocean currents in plankton
beds. Those that don't get eaten eventually make
it close to shore, where they settle into the rich
mud of estuaries and tide pools to grow to the
juvenile stage—the stage at which most of them
are harvested and eaten. Those who do make it to
adulthood swim out to the open ocean, where they
mate and die—about a year after their birth.

Farm-Raised Shrimp

According to the experts, wild and farmed shrimp taste remarkably alike—a good thing, since more than half of the shrimp eaten in the U.S. have been farmed. The two most popular farmed species are white shrimp from South America and black tiger shrimp from Asia. With modern shrimp-farming techniques, the larvae are maintained on land in shallow artificial ponds of seawater until they reach harvestable size, at about six months of age.

SHRIMP
IN THE
SPOTLIGHT

SPAGHETTI WITH GARLIC SLIVERS AND SHRIMP

This simple pasta was inspired by my favorite local Italian restaurant, Farfalle, in Los Angeles.

6 garlic cloves, peeled
1 pound medium shrimp, peeled
    and deveined
salt and freshly ground pepper
½ cup olive oil
¼ cup chopped fresh Italian parsley
juice of 1 lemon
1 pound spaghetti, cooked and drained

Bring a small pot of water to a boil, and blanch the garlic 2 minutes. Rinse with cold water and slice thinly.

Pat shrimp dry and season with salt and pepper. Heat half the oil in a large skillet over high heat. Sauté half the shrimp, turning frequently, until pink all over, and remove with a slotted spoon. Heat the remaining oil, and sauté the remaining shrimp. Remove with slotted spoon and reduce the heat to medium-low. Add the garlic, and cook until nearly golden. Return shrimp to the pan along with parsley and lemon juice. Season with salt and pepper, stir, and cook just to heat through. Pour over pasta in a bowl. Toss well and serve. Also delicious as a cold pasta salad.

SERVES 4

SHRIMP WITH ANCHOS AND GARLIC

Ancho chiles, available in Mexican markets and specialty stores, are dried poblanos. They are brown, wrinkly-skinned, and wide-shouldered, and add an interesting smoky flavor and chewy texture. Serve over rice to offset the strong, rich flavors.

1 pound large shrimp, peeled and deveined
salt and freshly ground pepper
¾ cup olive oil
10 garlic cloves, thinly sliced
1 to 2 dried ancho chiles, stemmed,
    seeded, and roughly chopped
¼ cup lime *or* lemon juice

Pat shrimp dry and season all over with salt and pepper. Heat the oil in a large skillet over high heat. Cook the shrimp until pink all over, about 1 minute per side. Remove with slotted spoon and set aside.

Reduce heat under pan to medium-low and let cool down. Add garlic and anchos. Cook, stirring frequently, until aroma is released, about 1 minute. Stir in lime juice and shrimp, cook an additional minute, and serve.

SERVES 4

SHRIMP AND LEEKS

This classic Chinese dish is stir-fried and then steamed for truly tender, sweet leeks.

1 pound large shrimp, peeled and
   deveined
1 tablespoon dry sherry
1½ teaspoons cornstarch
4 tablespoons peanut oil
2 teaspoons minced garlic
2 leeks, white and pale green parts
salt and freshly ground pepper
½ cup chicken stock
¼ teaspoon sugar
1 teaspoon sesame oil

Stir together the shrimp, sherry, and cornstarch in a bowl, and refrigerate.

Heat 2 tablespoons of the peanut oil in a large skillet over high heat. Lift shrimp from the marinade, shaking off excess liquid, and add to pan. Stir-fry just until pink, about 2 minutes. Transfer to platter.

Add the remaining peanut oil to pan. Reduce heat to medium and add garlic, leeks, salt, and pepper. Stir-fry 1 minute. Pour in the chicken stock and sugar. Reduce heat to low, cover, and cook 10 minutes. Uncover, stir in the shrimp, and cook just to heat through. Serve hot.

SERVES 4

GRILLED SHRIMP WITH TOMATOES AND GARLIC

This elegant, easy dish also makes a good appetizer for a formal dinner.

8 jumbo shrimp, in the shell
3 tablespoons olive oil
salt and freshly ground pepper
3 garlic cloves, chopped
2 tablespoons chopped fresh basil
½ cup dry white wine
8 plum tomatoes, seeded and diced

Preheat the grill or broiler.

Slice the shrimp lengthwise along the inside curve to butterfly, leaving shells on. Brush with oil, and season with salt and pepper. Broil or grill, shells to the flame, 3 to 4 minutes.

Meanwhile, heat the remaining oil in a medium skillet over medium heat. Briefly sauté the garlic. Add the basil and wine, and simmer about 2 minutes. Stir in the tomatoes and cook an additional 3 minutes. Season to taste with salt and pepper.

Divide the shrimp and arrange on 2 serving plates. Spoon on the sauce and serve hot.

SERVES 2

COCONUT CURRY SHRIMP

Serve this fragrant stew over rice for instant weeknight gratification.

2 tablespoons butter
1 large onion, chopped
salt and freshly ground pepper
1 tablespoon minced garlic
2 teaspoons fresh grated ginger
1 serrano chile, seeded and minced
½ teaspoon curry powder
¼ teaspoon turmeric
¼ teaspoon sugar
1 cup low-fat coconut milk
1 pound extra-large shrimp, peeled
  and deveined

Melt the butter in a large skillet over medium-high heat. Sauté the onion with salt and pepper until lightly browned. Turn the heat to high and stir in garlic, ginger, serrano, curry, turmeric, and sugar. Cook less than 1 minute, just to release aromas. Pour in coconut milk and bring to a boil.

Season the shrimp all over with salt and pepper. Add the shrimp to the pan and reduce to a simmer. Cook, uncovered, turning the shrimp once, about 5 minutes. Test shrimp for doneness, adjust seasonings with salt and pepper, and serve hot.

SERVES 2 TO 4

PASTA ARRABIATA
WITH SHRIMP

For those who love spicy tomato sauce and pasta, a sure crowd-pleaser.

3 tablespoons olive oil
1 pound large shrimp, peeled
  and deveined
salt and freshly ground pepper
1 tablespoon minced garlic
1 teaspoon red pepper flakes
1 (28-ounce) can crushed tomatoes
2 tablespoons chopped fresh basil
  or parsley
1 pound linguine or penne pasta,
  cooked and drained

Heat 2 tablespoons of the oil in a large nonstick skillet over high heat. Season the shrimp all over with salt and pepper. Sauté until pink all over, about 2 minutes. Transfer with slotted spoon to platter.

Reduce the heat under the skillet to medium-low and add remaining oil. Add garlic and red pepper flakes, and cook, stirring frequently, until aroma is released, about 1 minute. Pour in tomatoes, season with salt and pepper, and simmer over low heat, uncovered, about 15 minutes to thicken. Stir in shrimp, with their accumulated juices, and basil, and remove from heat. Pour over pasta in a bowl. Toss and serve.

SERVES 4

THAI SHRIMP PIZZA

A California pizza if ever there was one—inspired by the gang at California Pizza Kitchens.

¼ cup olive oil
1 teaspoon dried red chile flakes
6 large shrimp, peeled, deveined,
   and halved lengthwise
2 (5-ounce) pizza dough balls
   or prepared crust
½ cup shredded mozzarella cheese
¼ cup shredded fontina cheese
1 zucchini, seeded and julienned
½ red bell pepper, seeded and julienned
2 teaspoons chopped fresh mint
1 thin slice red onion, in rings
juice of 1 lime

In a small bowl, combine olive oil and chile flakes. Add shrimp, and marinate at room temperature up to 1 hour.

If using fresh dough, preheat oven to 515 degrees F with a pizza stone in place. Follow package directions for prepared crust.

Roll out dough on lightly floured pizza paddle. Brush lightly with oil from the marinade. Combine the 2 cheeses and spread all but about $\frac{1}{4}$ cup evenly over the dough, leaving edges bare for crust. Arrange the zucchini and red pepper strips, and top with the shrimp. Sprinkle with mint, red onion, and remaining cheese. Transfer to the oven and bake until cheese is melted and shrimp cooked, about 8 minutes. Remove, sprinkle with lime juice, and serve.

MAKES 2

STEAMED SHRIMP
WITH GARLIC

You can improvise a steamer by placing a small custard cup or ramekin upside down in a large pot and filling the pot with water to a depth of halfway up the ramekin. Place a plate, large enough to hold the shrimp but still allowing air to circulate around its edges, on top of the ramekin (a wok with steaming rack is excellent for this).

8 ounces jumbo shrimp, in the shell
2 tablespoons peanut oil
2 teaspoons minced garlic
1 tablespoon rice vinegar
1 tablespoon soy sauce

Butterfly the shrimp with the shell on by slicing in half lengthwise, along the inside curve, leaving tail end intact. Arrange on steamer plate, cut-side up.

In a small skillet, heat the peanut oil and garlic over medium heat, swirling occasionally, until the aroma is released. Drizzle over shrimp. Sprinkle with vinegar. Place over water in steamer and bring to a boil. Cover and cook 10 to 15 minutes, until shells are pink and shrimp opaque. Carefully remove hot plate, drizzle with soy sauce, and serve.

SERVES 2

SHRIMP WITH SNOW PEAS

Snow peas show off shrimp's delicacy in this classic Chinese stir-fry.

½ pound medium shrimp, peeled and deveined
2 teaspoons plus 2 tablespoons dry sherry
1 teaspoon cornstarch
3 tablespoons water
1 tablespoon soy sauce
½ teaspoon sugar
½ teaspoon salt
¼ teaspoon sesame oil
1 tablespoon peanut oil
2 teaspoons minced ginger
1 teaspoon minced garlic
2 scallions, thinly sliced
½ pound snow peas, trimmed and cut into ½-inch diagonal slices

Combine the shrimp, 2 teaspoons sherry, and cornstarch in a small bowl. Toss to coat evenly, and chill ½ hour.

Whisk together the 2 tablespoons dry sherry, water, soy sauce, sugar, salt, and sesame oil. Set aside for sauce.

Heat a large skillet or wok over high heat. Whirl in the peanut oil to coat. Add the shrimp (lifting from the marinade) and stir-fry just until pink, 1 to 2 minutes. Transfer to a platter. Add the ginger, garlic, and scallions to the hot pan, adding a few drops of oil if dry, and stir-fry less than 1 minute. Add snow peas and continue frying, stirring constantly, 1 to 2 minutes to soften. Pour in the sauce mixture and reserved shrimp, and cook 1 minute longer. Serve hot over rice.

SERVES 2 TO 4

SHRIMP OKRA GUMBO

A gumbo with some shortcuts: no roux or smoked pork products. Though it lacks the underlying smokiness of the real New Orleans thing, the flavor from these slowly cooked vegetables is quite delicious. (Substitute the fat from 4 strips of fried bacon in place of the oil for a touch of pork flavor.)

¼ cup vegetable oil
1½ pounds okra, trimmed and thinly sliced
2 onions, thinly sliced
2 green bell peppers, cored, seeded,
    and thinly sliced
1 celery rib, thinly sliced
1 quart fish stock or mixture of half water,
    half clam juice
3 large tomatoes, chopped
¼ teaspoon each black pepper, white pepper,
    cayenne, and paprika (or more to taste)
6 dashes Tabasco

3 tablespoons tomato paste
1 teaspoon salt
2 pounds medium shrimp, peeled
2 tablespoons cold butter
¼ teaspoon filé powder

Heat the oil in a large, heavy stockpot over medium-high heat. Sauté the okra, onions, green peppers, and celery 10 minutes. Add the fish stock, tomatoes, spices, Tabasco, tomato paste, and salt. Bring to a boil, reduce to a simmer, and cook, covered, 1 hour 20 minutes, until the broth is thick and the okra is tender.

Add the shrimp. Turn heat to medium-high and cook, uncovered, until shrimp are pink, about 2 minutes. Reduce heat to low and stir in butter, a tablespoon at a time, and filé. Adjust seasonings and serve hot over rice.

SERVES 4 TO 6

THE EASIEST SCAMPI

Shrimp and garlic is a marriage of tastes very few people can resist.

olive oil for coating
1 pound jumbo shrimp, in the shell
   and butterflied
salt and freshly ground pepper
1 stick butter
6 garlic cloves, peeled and minced
2 tablespoons dry white wine
1½ tablespoons chopped fresh
   Italian parsley
lemon wedges for garnish

Preheat the broiler and coat the rack with olive oil.

Arrange the butterflied shrimp shell-side up on the rack. Lightly brush with olive oil, and season with salt and pepper. Broil 4 minutes on one side and remove.

Melt the butter in a large skillet over medium-low heat. Cook the garlic until soft, about 3 minutes. Add the wine and simmer 2 minutes longer. Add the shrimp to the pan along with the parsley. Toss to coat evenly and cook 1 to 2 minutes. Serve hot with lemon wedges.

SERVES 2 TO 4

Shrimp by Number per Pound

40 plus	cocktail or bay size
35 to 40	medium
31 to 35	large
26 to 30	extra large
21 to 25	jumbo
16 to 20	super jumbo

Distributors classify shrimp by the number of pieces that make a pound. So "40 plus" means that there are over 40 pieces in a pound of cocktail shrimp. Another way to indicate count is to say, for instance, "under 20" for super jumbo, which means there are less than 20 shrimp to the pound.

When possible, purchase shrimp uncooked, with their shells on but their heads removed. Shrimp that have been peeled at the market will not keep as well, and the shells—which take only minutes to peel—offer more possibilities for cooking and stock-making.

Since only 2 percent of the shrimp sold in the United States are fresh, the shrimp that most of us encounter at the local market (unless we live along the Gulf) have arrived at the store frozen. Shrimp are sold in 5-pound frozen blocks to retailers, who then break off and thaw a few pounds at a time. Defrosted shrimp will keep, under refrigeration, for two to three days. As with most seafood, it is always best to purchase shrimp on the day you plan on cooking them and to refrigerate them until cooking time.

COLD SOBA NOODLES WITH SHRIMP AND SCALLIONS

Soba—the dried Japanese buckwheat and yam noodles that are so delicious to slurp in the summertime—and roasted seeweed or nori are now available in the international section at the supermarket.

4 ounces dried soba noodles
soy sauce for coating
½ pound medium shrimp, in the shell
3 tablespoons soy sauce
3 tablespoons rice wine vinegar
3 tablespoons mirin (sweet rice wine)
¼ teaspoon wasabi paste
7 scallions, trimmed and thinly sliced
1 sheet (about 7½" x 8½") roasted nori (seaweed)

Bring a large pot of salted water to a boil. Boil the noodles 3 minutes, drain, and rinse with cold water. Drain again and transfer to bowl. Toss with about 1 tablespoon of soy sauce to coat. Cover, and chill at least 4 hours.

When ready to serve, boil the shrimp in a medium saucepan of salted water 1 minute. Drain and set aside to cool. When cool enough to handle, peel the shrimp.

In a small bowl, stir together the soy sauce, vinegar, mirin, and wasabi. Pour over the noodles and toss. Transfer to a platter. Top with scallions, nori, and shrimp, and serve or refrigerate.

SERVES 2 TO 4

SHRIMP STEAMED IN SPICY BEER BROTH

This is a quick adaptation of the dish made in Los Angeles by the Killer Shrimp chain. Serve with plenty of bread, pasta, or rice for the delicious broth. Bibs are optional.

1 pound large shrimp, in the shell
3 tablespoons butter
1 (12-ounce) bottle beer
1 onion, chopped
1 teaspoon minced garlic
½ cup chopped tomatoes
¼ teaspoon dried red chile flakes
¼ teaspoon dried thyme
½ teaspoon dried rosemary, crumbled
salt and freshly ground pepper
2 cups fish stock

Peel the shrimp, keeping the shells. Devein, if desired, and refrigerate the shrimp.

Melt 1 tablespoon of the butter in a heavy, large saucepan over medium-high heat. Sauté the shells until pink, then pour in the beer. Cook at a boil until about ⅓ cup remains, about 15 minutes. Strain, pressing shells to extract liquid. Discard the shells.

Wipe the pot clean and melt the remaining 2 tablespoons of butter. Add the onion and garlic, and cook over medium heat until soft. Stir in the tomatoes, red chile flakes, thyme, rosemary, salt, and pepper; cook 2 minutes. Pour in stock and reserved beer liquid. Simmer 7 minutes. Stir in shrimp, and simmer until shrimp are done, about 3 minutes longer. Divide the shrimp, and ladle into bowls. Serve with crusty bread or steamed rice.

SERVES 2 TO 4

LIME-AND-CHILE
BARBECUED SHRIMP

*Shells are optional for this fiery grilled shrimp dish.
I prefer them left on for the added crunch and as
insurance against overcooking.*

½ cup lime juice
1 tablespoon prepared Vietnamese chile sauce
¼ cup olive oil
salt
1 pound jumbo shrimp, in the shell
prepared pineapple or mango salsa for serving

In a shallow bowl, whisk together lime juice,
chile sauce, olive oil, and salt. Add shrimp, toss
to coat evenly and marinate at room temperature 15 minutes or in the refrigerator 1 hour.

To cook, preheat the grill or broiler.

Thread each skewer with 4 shrimp. Place on
broiler rack or grill and cook 7 minutes total,
turning occasionally. Serve hot with cold salsa.

SERVES 4

The Family of Shrimp

All 300 species of shrimp in the world share certain characteristics. All are 10-legged crustaceans from the phylum arthropoda, with exterior skeletons that they shed in order to grow. Each shrimp's papery shell consists of 38 segments.

Shrimp are classified according to habitat: warm water, cold water, freshwater, rock, and sand. Some of the most popular species on the American table are white, pink, brown, and tiger shrimp. (A shrimp called "green" is a shrimp that is uncooked.) Since most of us purchase our shrimp according to what is available in the market by size rather than type, learning to differentiate the types is not a priority.

Prawns are classified by the U.S. Department of Agriculture as a type of freshwater shrimp from Hawaii. Informally in the U.S., the word "prawn" is often used by restaurateurs to denote the very largest, prime shrimp. In the rest of the English-speaking world, shrimp are commonly called "prawns."

TEMPURA SHRIMP

Try strips of bell pepper, mushrooms, broccoli, and cauliflowerettes, slices of squash, carrots, and other root vegetables for a traditional tempura dinner.

1 pound jumbo shrimp, peeled and
   butterflied along inside curve,
   with tail on
¾ cup ice-cold water
1 cup prepared tempura batter mix
peanut or vegetable oil for frying

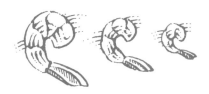

Wash and pat shrimp dry and refrigerate.

Pour the cold water into a bowl, and add tempura mix. Lightly whisk until flour disappears.

Pour oil to a depth of 2 inches into deep pot and bring to deep-fry temperature, 350 degrees F. Holding shrimp by tail, dip into batter to coat, and shake off excess. Slide into hot oil and fry until golden all over, about 3 minutes. Transfer with slotted spoon to paper towels to drain. Serve hot with dipping sauce and tempura vegetables, if desired.

SERVES 4

FRIED SHRIMP
NEW ORLEANS STYLE

Spicy beer-battered shrimp can be used as a sandwich filling. For an authentic po' boy, slather an Italian roll with remoulade or a spicy mayonnaise, plenty of shredded lettuce, and thinly sliced lemon to cut the richness.

½ cup all-purpose flour
¼ cup cornmeal
½ teaspoon baking powder
1 teaspoon salt
1 teaspoon sugar
½ teaspoon cayenne
⅛ teaspoon cinnamon
¾ cup warm beer
vegetable oil for frying
1 pound medium shrimp, peeled,
    with tails on

In a mixing bowl, combine flour, cornmeal, baking powder, salt, sugar, cayenne, and cinnamon. Pour in beer and whisk until smooth. Let sit on a counter 1 hour.

To cook, pour oil to a depth of 2 inches into deep pot or fryer and bring to deep-fry temperature, 350 degrees F. Add the shrimp a small handful at a time to the batter. Lift out, shake off excess, and carefully drop into hot oil. Fry until browned all over, about 2 minutes. Transfer with slotted spoon to paper towels to drain. Serve hot with any of the cold dipping sauces or honey mustard.

SERVES 4

SHRIMP WITH
FRESH HERBS AND PERNOD

A simple dish such as this is a great showcase for the sweet delicacy of shrimp. Serve with good bread and premixed salad for a quick weeknight treat.

4 tablespoons butter
½ pound extra-large shrimp, peeled
  and deveined
salt and freshly ground pepper
2 tomatoes, peeled, seeded, and diced
½ cup chopped fresh herbs such as basil,
  parsley, chives, and tarragon
2 tablespoons Pernod *or* other
  anise-flavored liqueur

Melt 2 tablespoons of the butter in a medium skillet over medium-high heat. Pat the shrimp dry and season all over with salt and pepper. Sauté just until pink all over, about 2 minutes. Remove with slotted spoon to platter.

Reduce the heat to medium and add tomatoes and herbs. Season with salt and pepper, and simmer 5 minutes. Reduce heat to low. Stir in remaining butter, Pernod, and shrimp, and cook about 1 minute until sauce is smooth and shrimp heated through. Serve hot.

SERVES 2

CONVERSIONS

LIQUID
1Tbsp = 15 ml
½ cup = 4 fl oz = 125 ml
1 cup = 8 fl oz = 250 ml

DRY
¼ cup = 4 Tbsp = 2 oz = 60 g
1 cup = ½ pound = 8 oz = 250 g

FLOUR
½ cup = 60 g
1 cup = 4 oz = 125 g

TEMPERATURE
400° F = 200° C = gas mark 6
375° F = 190° C = gas mark 5
350° F = 175° C = gas mark 4

MISCELLANEOUS
2 Tbsp butter = 1 oz = 30 g
1 inch = 2.5 cm
all-purpose flour = plain flour
baking soda = bicarbonate of soda
brown sugar = demerara sugar